The Ultimate Guide Hurling

GW00992556

Gavin Mortimer

This book was conceived, edited and designed for Gill & Macmillan by
Tony Potter Publishing Ltd
tonypotter.com

Illustrators: John Cooper & Brett Hudson
Editorial consultants: Noel Quinlan & Les Fitzmaurice
Layouts: Sue Rose
All photos © www.inpho.ie

GILL & MACMILLAN
Hume Avenue, Park West, Dublin 12
with associated companies throughout the world
www.gillmacmillan.ie

978 07171 4592 8

First published 2009

Contents

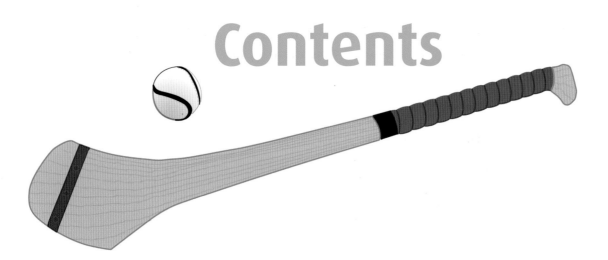

Let's Get Hurling!

Henry Shefflin

There's no other game in the world like hurling, a sport that requires speed, strength and skilful stickwork. It's fast and furious and the fans can't get enough of it. That's why this book is devoted to hurling's heroes, past and present.

Limerick fans enjoy the game

The Ultimate Guide to Hurling is the book to have if you're mad about the sport. Discover hurling's wonderful history, from the origins of the game to the stars of today such as 'King' Henry Shefflin and Dan 'the Man' Shanahan!

Learn how to become a hotshot with a hurley with our easy-to-follow guides that give you the lowdown on all the skills such as striking, catching and lifting. You'll also discover that hurling has its very own language. There are some amazing facts and stats from the game: the record-breakers, the All-Stars and, of course, all the action from the All-Ireland Championship.

Hurling is a game with a rich history and a bright future. So don't delay, turn the page and find out what makes hurling such a great sport!

Hurling's Heartland

Hurling is played in all of Ireland's 32 counties, although its heart beats most strongly in Tipperary, Cork and Kilkenny which have won an amazing 86 of the 109 All-Ireland Championships between them. It remains very much a rural game and only Cork and Waterford can be described as hurling cities.

Galway: The Tribesmen play in maroon and white shirts and have won four All-Ireland titles.

Clare: The Banner County play in yellow and blue shirts and have won three All-Ireland titles.

Kerry: The Kingdom play in green and gold shirts and have won one All-Ireland title.

GALWAY

CLARE

LIMERICK

KERRY

TIPPERARY

CORK

WATERFORD

Cork: The Rebel County play in red shirts and have won 30 All-Ireland titles.

Limerick: The Treaty County play in green shirts and have won seven All-Ireland titles.

Waterford: The Crystal County play in white shirts and have won two All-Ireland titles.

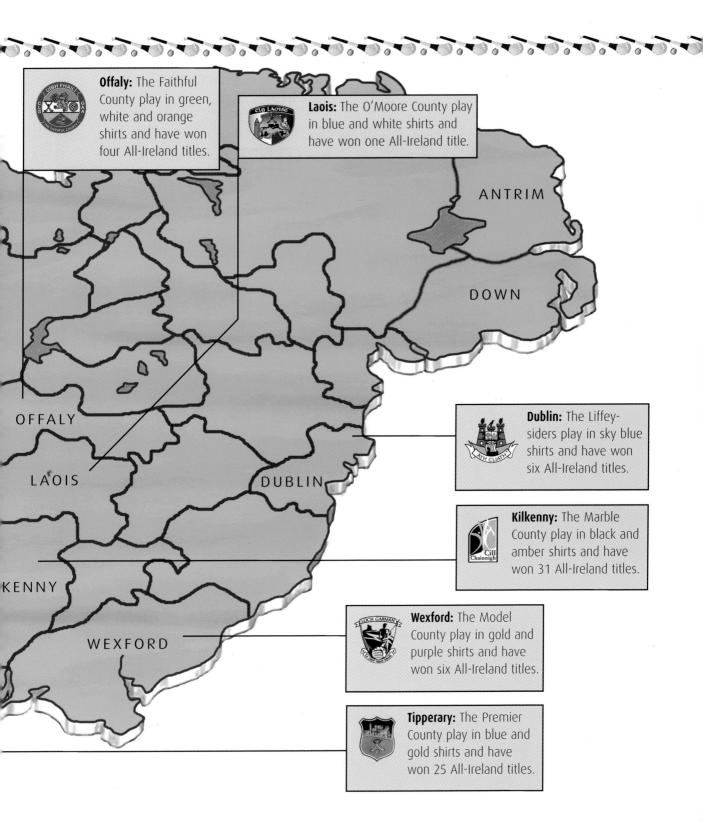

Offaly: The Faithful County play in green, white and orange shirts and have won four All-Ireland titles.

Laois: The O'Moore County play in blue and white shirts and have won one All-Ireland title.

ANTRIM

DOWN

OFFALY

LAOIS

DUBLIN

Dublin: The Liffey-siders play in sky blue shirts and have won six All-Ireland titles.

Kilkenny: The Marble County play in black and amber shirts and have won 31 All-Ireland titles.

KENNY

WEXFORD

Wexford: The Model County play in gold and purple shirts and have won six All-Ireland titles.

Tipperary: The Premier County play in blue and gold shirts and have won 25 All-Ireland titles.

Field of Glory

Each team consists of 15 players – a goalkeeper and 14 outfield players. The goalkeeper wears a different-coloured jersey to his team-mates.

Senior Championship matches last for 70 minutes (two halves of 35 minutes) while other matches go on for 60 minutes.

The average hurling field is 137m long and 82m wide with goalposts at each end. The posts are in the shape of a letter 'H' with a net attached to the bottom half.

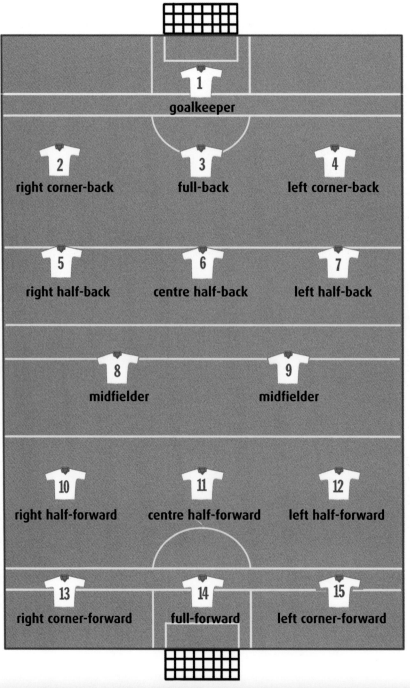

1 goalkeeper

2 right corner-back   3 full-back   4 left corner-back

5 right half-back   6 centre half-back   7 left half-back

8 midfielder   9 midfielder

10 right half-forward   11 centre half-forward   12 left half-forward

13 right corner-forward   14 full-forward   15 left corner-forward

Mark Keane scores a penalty

Eight officials watch over a hurling match – a referee, two linesmen, a sideline official and four umpires (two at each end).

A player can score a goal either with his hurley or his foot, or by striking the sliotar in flight with his hand. But he is not permitted to carry the sliotar into the net.

In front of each goal are two rectangles marked on the pitch, one bigger than the other. The goalkeeper may not be charged when he is in the small rectangle, but he can be challenged for possession of the sliotar.

If the defending team commits an aggressive foul in the large rectangle, then the attacking team is awarded a penalty puck *(see How to Speak Hurling, p36).* If the offence is a technical foul then the referee awards the attacking side a free puck from the centre of the 20m line.

There are many technical fouls but some of the most common are to overcarry the sliotar, to interfere with an opponent's hurley in the air, and to toss the sliotar with the hand and catch it without playing it with the hurley. Aggressive fouls include striking an opponent with the hurley or kicking him.

The sliotar may be struck with the hurley when it's on the ground or in the air, but players are forbidden from touching the sliotar with their hands when it is on the ground. Players can carry the sliotar in the hand for a maximum of four consecutive steps before they must release it, but there is no limit to the number of steps allowed if the sliotar is balanced on or hopping on the hurley.

What's the score?

There are two ways to score in hurling. A goal is scored when a team plays the sliotar over the goal-line between the two posts and under the crossbar. This is worth three points. If the sliotar goes over the bar and between the posts then one point is scored.

The scoreline reflects both scores and the goals always come first. For example, Cork 0–20 Tipperary 3–13 means Cork scored no goals and 20 points but Tipperary scored 3 goals (worth 3 points each) plus 13 points giving them a total of 22. The team with the highest combined total wins the match.

The Dream Team

NO. 1

Damien Fitzhenry

Goalkeeper

WEXFORD

Along with nine of his brothers, Fitzhenry played hurling and football for Duffry Rovers in his youth, while three of his sisters represented the club in camogie.

Having risen up through the U21 ranks of the Wexford panel, Fitzhenry made his senior debut for the county in 1993. Three years later he was between the posts as Wexford beat Limerick to win their first All-Ireland title since 1968.

The following season, 1997, Fitzhenry helped Wexford to the Leinster crown and he was rewarded with his first All-Star award.

In 2001 Fitzhenry hit the headlines when he scored two goals for Wexford in the All-Ireland quarter-final against Limerick, one from a penalty and one from a free. He picked up his second All-Star award in 2004 and the fabulous Fitzhenry remains one of the best goalkeepers in the game.

[False: He's the youngest of fifteen]

HAVE A HIT!

True or False?
Damien is the oldest of fifteen children.

Damien Fitzhenry is a super shot-stopper

10

Goalkeeping Greats

The forwards get the goals, the midfielders get the glory but it's the goalkeepers who can keep their team in the game with a great save.

Look back at some of the great matches in hurling history and you'll find that it was the goalkeepers who won the match for their team just as much as the players who picked up the points.

Kilkenny beat Cork in the 1947 All-Ireland final thanks to some spectacular saves by Jim Donegan, while Wexford triumphed over Tipperary in 1968 because of Pat Nolan's reflexes. Offaly were only able to defeat Galway in 1981 because Damien Martin batted away a strike late on in the game.

First and foremost, a goalkeeping great must have excellent reflexes and be able to react quickly when an opponent strikes for goal. Good eyesight helps too, because in a crowded rectangle it's not easy to judge the flight of a fiercely-struck shot.

Where possible, always try to catch the sliotar rather than bat it away because there might be an opponent lurking close by to lash the rebound into the net.

You also need to be decisive, and sometimes even bossy! Work with your defenders to repel opposition attacks and tell them if they are not marking their forwards properly. You should also tell them if you're going for the sliotar. Shout 'Goalkeeper's sliotar!' so they know you're coming.

The other crucial skill a goalkeeper needs is the puck-out because with one clean strike you can send the sliotar deep into the opposition half.

Tipperary goalkeeper Brendan Cummins won three All-Star awards

In the final seconds of the 1956 All-Ireland final Wexford keeper Art Foley prevented a winning Cork goal from Christy Ring with a brilliant save that even Ring applauded!

11

Get a Grip!

The hurley is the tool of the trade, the piece of wood that makes hurling such a super sport.

The ball is called a sliotar. It must weigh between 100–130g and be between 23–25cm in circumference. Its core is made of cork, which is then bound by layers of thread and finally covered in pigskin leather.

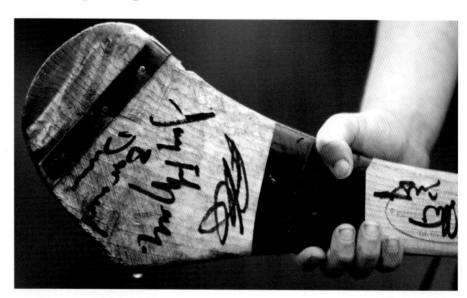

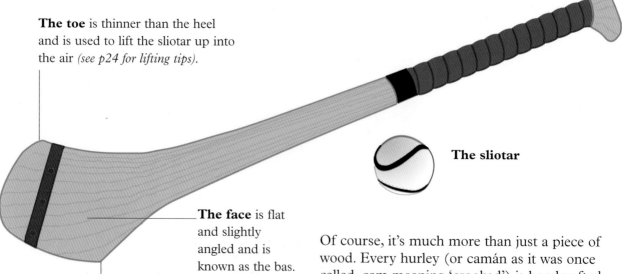

The toe is thinner than the heel and is used to lift the sliotar up into the air *(see p24 for lifting tips)*.

The sliotar

The face is flat and slightly angled and is known as the bas. It's used to strike the sliotar.

The heel is the thickest part of the hurley and is used to give the sliotar height when striking it from the ground.

Of course, it's much more than just a piece of wood. Every hurley (or camán as it was once called, cam meaning 'crooked') is handcrafted from the root of the ash tree. Why ash? Because it is a very flexible wood and can withstand the clash of hurleys better than other woods. Most hurleys are between 64–97cm in length and the face must not be more than 13cm in width.

To get the correct grip, balance the hurley on the palm of your weaker hand and close your fingers around the end near the bas. Lower your stronger hand over the top of the handle and close your fingers. The grip shown below is a right-handed position.

The lock position

In the ready position, slide the weaker hand up the handle to lock with the dominant hand at the top of the hurley. This is the lock position and is very important in learning how to strike the sliotar.

The ready position

Stand with your feet shoulder-width apart with your stronger hand holding the hurley at the top of the handle and the weaker hand holding the handle three quarters of the way down.

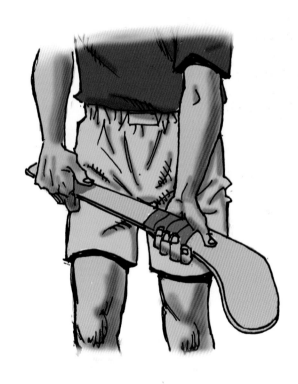

The lifting position

In the ready position, open your weaker hand. Use the thumb of your stronger hand to turn the hurley so its toe is pointing away from your body. Close the thumb of your weaker hand so both thumbs are pointing towards the bas. Now you're ready to lift the sliotar into the air (see p24).

Take Strike

Now you can handle the hurley, you're ready to learn how to strike the sliotar straight and true!

Let's begin with the sliotar on the ground – the easiest start! Stand in the ready position with your front foot in line with the sliotar. Move your weaker hand up the handle to the lock position *(see p13 for a reminder)* and with a slight bend of your knees, swing the hurley at the sliotar. It should be the flat bas of the hurley that makes contact with the sliotar. Remember, your eyes should be watching the sliotar, not where you want it to go!

When striking the sliotar from the hand it is important to stand side-on to where you want the sliotar to go. Hold the sliotar in your weaker hand and toss it up to shoulder height. Bring your hands into the lock position straightaway and raise the hurley so the bas is above your head. Then, take a step forward and swing the hurley as it descends, hitting the sliotar when it's about thigh height.

The hardest strike to master is the overhead one, but the key is to always keep your eye on the sliotar as it approaches. Get underneath the sliotar as it drops and move your hands into the lock position. Swing the hurley at the sliotar when it is at the highest point above your head, and roll your wrists and shoulders to direct the strike. Don't worry if you miss at first – with practice you'll be able to time the strike much better!

top tip

Always remember to follow through with your hurley once you've struck the sliotar.

Notice how Shane McGrath is side-on with the bas above his head and his hands in lock position

The Dream Team

NO. 3

Diarmuid O'Sullivan

Full-back

CORK

Known as 'The Rock', Diarmuid O'Sullivan has been one of hurling's hotshots for over ten years, ever since he won the Cork Senior Hurling Championship with Imokilly in 1997. O'Sullivan won an All-Ireland medal with the Cork U21 team in the same year, and he was soon selected for the senior side.

He was part of the 'Rebels' side which won the Munster title in 1999 and a few months later O'Sullivan was at the heart of the Cork defence as they defeated Kilkenny to claim their first All-Ireland title since 1990. 'The Rock' capped an amazing 1999 by also picking up his first All-Star award and being named Young Hurler of the Year.

O'Sullivan tasted more All-Ireland success with Cork in 2004 and 2005, and has a deserved reputation as one of the finest full-backs of recent years.

Diarmuid is a rock in defence

HAVE A HIT!

True or False?
Diarmuid won a Munster Football Championship medal with Cork in 2002.

[True]

Be a Top Tackler

You need a big heart to be a hit at hurling, especially when it comes to tackling.

Waterford close down Cork's Steven White

The shoulder-to-shoulder clash

Move in close to your opponent so that your shoulder and hip are in contact with his, but remember to look at the sliotar and not at him. Ensuring that one foot stays on the ground at all times (otherwise it's a foul against you), raise the hurley and swing for the sliotar with a quick flick of the wrists.

The shoulder-to-shoulder charge

This tackle is more aggressive than the clash and allows you to charge the player in possession of the sliotar side-on. Again, at least one foot must be in contact with the ground.

The ground flick

As you approach your opponent keep your eyes on the sliotar. As you move in close, release your weaker hand from the hurley and with your dominant hand reach out with the hurley. With a strong swing of your wrist, flick the sliotar from your opponent. Stay close to your opponent as you perform the action to avoid being accidentally hit from their swing.

The frontal ground block

Step towards your opponent as he approaches and, taking the weaker hand off the hurley, extend your dominant hand so that the hurley is in front or behind the sliotar. Keep the hurley vertical and place one foot behind it for support, if necessary.

The frontal air block

As your opponent throws the sliotar from their hand to strike, step forward and bend your front knee at the same time. Reach forward with both hands close together on the hurley so that the bas is above your head (out of the way of your opponent's hurley). As your opponent is about to strike, use your hurley to block down on the sliotar and his hurley.

Deadly Defenders

Big, brave and bold – the key characteristics that a deadly defender needs. All this on top of their skill with a stick!

There are six defenders on a hurling team, but it doesn't matter if you're a left corner-back or a right half-back, the requirements are just the same.

Firstly, you need to be able to tackle – and tackle hard so that you win the sliotar from the opposition forward. That means you need courage and timing so that you don't give away a foul as you go for the sliotar *(see p16 for tips)*.

You also need confidence, particularly under a dropping sliotar which you know is going to attract the attention of several goal-hungry opponents! One of the masters of securing the dropping sliotar was Tipperary's Mick Roche in the 1960s. His rock-like presence under the high sliotar helped the Premier County to three All-Ireland titles.

But Roche didn't just catch the dropping sliotar, he always made great sweeping clearances, relieving the pressure on his goal and creating scoring opportunities for his forwards at the other end of the field.

Finally, look at some of the crack defenders in the game today – players such as Frank Lohan and Michael Kavanagh never take their eye off the man they're marking, even if the sliotar is at the other end of the field. Every deadly defender has great awareness of all that is going on around him. This means that he's never caught out of position!

Frank Lohan (left) clearing the danger

Traditionally there are regional variations in the design of the hurley. For example, the hurley used in Galway and Wexford has a chunkier bas than the one used in Tipperary and Kilkenny, while the Clare hurley is slightly longer than the Cork one.

The Dream Team

NO. 4

Eamon Buckley

Left corner-back

TIPPERARY

The flame-haired left corner-back is one of the rising stars in the hurling world, having learned his trade at the Drom-Inch club. In 2003 he enjoyed success with the Tipperary U21 side winning a Munster medal. Two years later Buckley made his senior debut for Tipp in the National Hurling League.

His championship debut came in 2007 against Limerick and Buckley has gone from strength to strength ever since, establishing himself as a thorn in the side of opposition forwards.

NO. 2

Frank Lohan

Right corner-back

CLARE

Hurling runs in the family as far as Frank Lohan is concerned. His father, Gus, played for Clare in the 1970s and his brother, Brian, was a favourite with The Banner faithful for a decade until his retirement in 2006.

Frank and Brian were both rock solid in defence when Clare won the All-Ireland title in 1995 for the first time in 81 years, and the brilliant brothers were no less influential in 1997 when Clare again lifted the Liam McCarthy Cup.

Frank won his first All-Star in 1999 and in recent years has captained his county.

[True]

HAVE A HIT!

True or False?
Frank and Brian Lohan are one of fifteen sets of brothers who have won hurling All-Stars.

Hurley Burley

Top facts and stats from the world of hurling.

The 1890 All-Ireland final was never completed because the Cork players walked off in protest at Wexford's rough play. The GAA backed Cork and gave them the title.

Waterford reached the 2008 All-Ireland final despite losing to Clare in the first round of the Munster Championship. The Crystal County entered the All-Ireland Qualifier Series and made it all the way to Croke Park under new manager, Davy Fitzgerald.

The Liam McCarthy Cup is awarded to the All-Ireland champions

The 1960 All-Ireland final between Wexford and Tipperary ended in chaos when the crowd mistook a free for the final whistle. Three of the Tipp players dashed off the pitch and when order had been restored they couldn't be found, so their side played the last minute with only 12 players. Luckily Wexford were already way ahead!

John Flanagan was an Olympic great, winning the hammer-throwing gold medal for the USA in 1900, 1904 and 1908. But big John was actually from Kilmallock and before emigrating had played for Munster hurlers.

The big prize in hurling is the Liam McCarthy Cup but the second tier competition (for teams ranked from 13 to 22) is called the Christy Ring Cup and sides ranked 23–32 compete for the Nicky Rackard Cup.

Stamford Bridge is normally associated with English soccer side Chelsea, but Munster played Leinster at the stadium in an 1896 hurling match. The game was a curtain-raiser to an England vs Ireland soccer match (which Ireland won!).

Arguably the most successful All-Ireland star was Pierce Grace. He won three hurling medals with Kilkenny from 1911 to 1913, having won two football medals with Dublin in 1906 and 1907.

Cork's James Kelleher achieved a first for a goalkeeper in the 1905 All-Ireland final against Kilkenny when his puck-out bounced over the bar for a score.

Des Foley of Dublin holds a special place in GAA folklore for being the only man to play for his province's hurlers and footballers in the finals of the Railway Cup...on the same day! Des did the double in 1962, and what's more he picked up a pair of winners' medals!

The All-Ireland semi-final between Kilkenny and Galway in 1926, broadcast by 2RN, was the first field sports radio commentary in Europe.

Offaly won the All-Ireland title in 1998 and also won their place in the history books by becoming the first county to lift the crown, having first lost in the Leinster provincial final.

Few hurlers can match the achievements of Cork's Jack Lynch. He won six All-Ireland medals in the 1940s and then went on to serve two terms as Taoiseach in the 1970s.

The first dismissal in an All-Ireland final happened in the very first year (1887) when a Galway hurler was given his marching orders for a trip. Luckily for him, history failed to record his name!

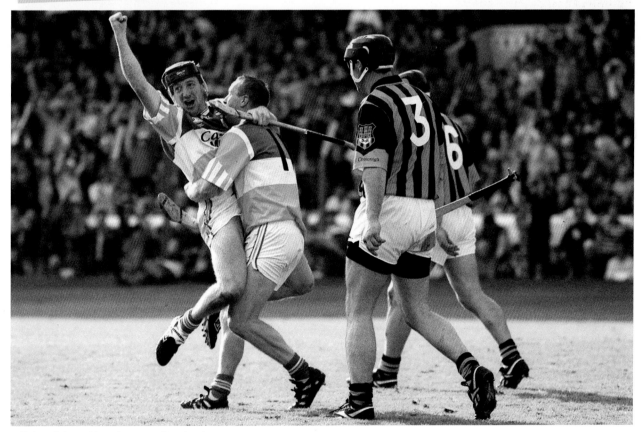

Offaly celebrate their historic All-Ireland win in 1998

Corking Cork

Cathal Naughton and Jerry O'Connor celebrate a Cork victory in 2008

The Rebels, County Cork, were the first county to win 30 All-Ireland finals and they remain the only side to have won four titles on the trot.

In 1941 Cork won the first of what would turn out to be a record run of All-Ireland triumphs. On the Rebel side against Dublin that day was a young forward who scored three points – his name was Christy Ring and he would become the greatest player ever to wear the famous red shirt.

Dublin were defeated again in the 1942 final and, in 1943, Cork thrashed Antrim 5–6 to 0–4. That made it three-in-a-row, a feat that the county had achieved once before in the 1890s. But in the 1944 final against Dublin, Cork went one better and won a record fourth successive title.

In the 1950s Cork won another three titles in a row – with Christy Ring at the height of his magic powers – and they repeated the hat-trick between 1976 and 1978 thanks to the likes of Jimmy Barry-Murphy, Seanie O'Leary and John Horgan.

Cork came close to a treble triumph this decade, winning the All-Ireland final in 2004 and 2005 with Jerry O'Connor and

Seán Óg Ó hAilpín in spell-binding form, but just losing out to Kilkenny in 2006. Don't bet against the Rebels racking up another three-in-a-row in the not too distant future!

The Tipperary defensive line of the late 1950s featuring John Doyle, Mick Maher and Kieran Carey was dubbed 'Hell's Kitchen' because they made life so unpleasant for opposition forwards!

The Dream Team

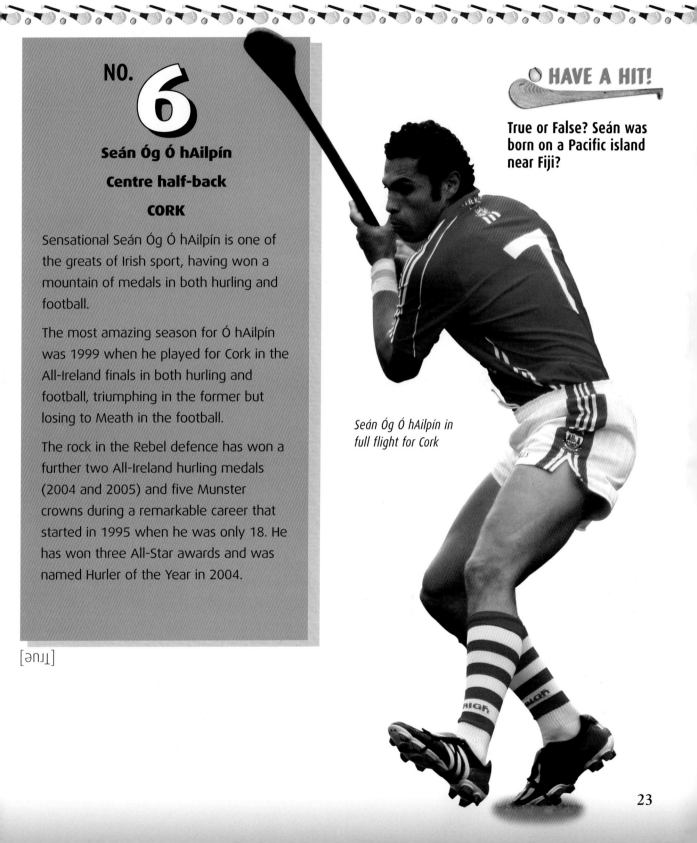

NO. 6

Seán Óg Ó hAilpín

Centre half-back

CORK

Sensational Seán Óg Ó hAilpín is one of the greats of Irish sport, having won a mountain of medals in both hurling and football.

The most amazing season for Ó hAilpín was 1999 when he played for Cork in the All-Ireland finals in both hurling and football, triumphing in the former but losing to Meath in the football.

The rock in the Rebel defence has won a further two All-Ireland hurling medals (2004 and 2005) and five Munster crowns during a remarkable career that started in 1995 when he was only 18. He has won three All-Star awards and was named Hurler of the Year in 2004.

Seán Óg Ó hAilpín in full flight for Cork

○ HAVE A HIT!

True or False? Seán was born on a Pacific island near Fiji?

[True]

We Have Lift Off!

Hurling isn't just about hitting the sliotar as hard as you can. Often a soft touch is required, such as when lifting the sliotar off the ground.

There are two ways to lift the sliotar with the hurley – the roll lift and the jab lift. Here's how to master both skills:

The roll lift

Place your weaker foot in line with the sliotar with your knees bent and your head over the sliotar. Keep the hurley parallel to the ground and place the toe of the hurley on the sliotar.

Roll the sliotar quickly towards you and slide the toe of the hurley under the sliotar to lift it.

When performing the roll lift both thumbs should point towards the bas of the hurley.

Take your weaker hand off the hurley with the fingers cupped and catch the sliotar as it's in the air.

The jab lift

Adopt the same position as for the roll lift, placing the toe of the hurley on the sliotar.

With the hurley parallel to the ground, slide the toe under the sliotar and lift it from the ground.

Take the weaker hand off the hurley and catch the sliotar as it's in the air.

Don't forget, if you pick up the sliotar with your hands it's a foul, and a ticking off from the referee!

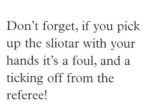

The Dream Team

NO. 5

Tommy Walsh

Right half-back

KILKENNY

One of the most versatile players in the game today, the talented Tommy Walsh has won four All-Star awards in four different positions – all before his 24th birthday!

His preferred position for Kilkenny is left half-back. He made his senior debut for the Marble County in 2003 and collected his first All-Ireland medal that same season in the victory over Cork.

In 2006 Walsh was part of the Kilkenny treble-winning side – securing the National Hurling League title, the Leinster crown and the Liam McCarthy Cup. He tasted further All-Ireland success in 2007 and 2008.

NO. 7

Ken McGrath

Left half-back

WATERFORD

With Waterford legend Pat McGrath as a father, it's no surprise that Ken is a chip off the old block with a reputation as one of the best catchers in the game.

The Deise dynamo made his senior debut aged just 17 and was a member of the side which won the Munster title in 2002 – their first provincial crown since 1963. Two years later, in 2004, McGrath skippered Waterford to another Munster title but hopes of All-Ireland glory were dashed in the semi-final.

In 2007 Waterford beat Kilkenny to win a National Hurling League medal and McGrath was named Man of the Match, another honour to go with his three All-Star awards.

Ken McGrath is a Waterford wonder

The Cool Cats

Kilkenny have been the cream of the All-Ireland Championship in recent years.

Kilkenny won the first All-Ireland title of the new millennium when they thrashed Offaly in 2000. Since then they have added another five victories to make them the most successful side of the decade.

Their very first All-Ireland triumph was in 1904 when Dick Doyle scored the crucial goal in the defeat of fierce rivals Cork. In the next ten years they achieved six more titles, including three-in-a-row from 1911 to 1913.

The next great Kilkenny side was in the 1930s when they scooped four All-Ireland medals, with a team which included legendary heroes Paddy Phelan and Lory Meagher. Although they continued to win championships over the next thirty years, it wasn't until the late 1960s that the Cats began to dominate the game once more.

Between 1969 and 1975 they won four titles and also produced some of the finest players in the history of the game, such as goalkeeper Noel Skehan and the fantastic forward Eddie Keher.

It was another goalscoring great, DJ Carey, who helped Kilkenny win the 2000 title with a 2–4 tally. With modern day hurling heroes such as Henry Shefflin, James Fitzpatrick and Tommy Walsh in their ranks it looks certain that the Cats' claws will remain sharp for years to come!

Kilkenny lift the 2008 Leinster trophy

Kilkenny's defeat of Waterford in the 2008 All-Ireland final surpassed the record of 30 victories held by Cork.

Timeline

1366: Hurling is banned by the Statute of Kilkenny because 'great evils' have been caused by the game.

1884: The Gaelic Athletic Association (GAA) is formed in a Thurles hotel by Michael Cusack and six other Irishmen.

1887: In the first All-Ireland final Tipperary, represented by Thurles, beat Galway 1–1 to 0–0, in front of 5,000 spectators.

1892: Teams are reduced from 21-a-side to 17-a-side and a goal is worth five points.

1895: Tipperary beat Kilkenny in the first All-Ireland final to be played on the present day site of Croke Park (then known as Jones's Road).

1896: A goal is reduced from five to three points and Tipperary thrash Dublin 8–14 to 0–4 in the most one-sided All-Ireland final ever.

1910: Seats are provided for the first time at Croke Park for 700 spectators during the All-Ireland final.

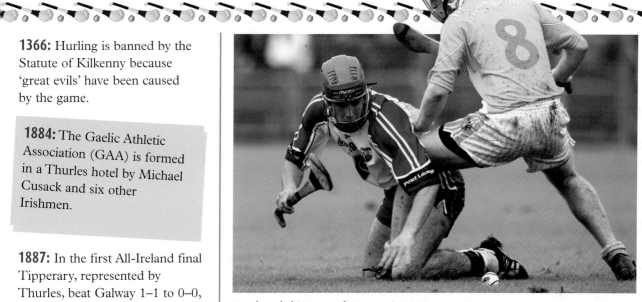
Numbered shirts were first worn in 1923

1913: Teams are reduced from 17-a-side to 15-a-side and counties adopt their own colours to wear.

1923: Players wear numbered jerseys for the first time.

1925: The National League competition begins and Cork are its first winners.

1944: Cork beat Dublin to win their fourth consecutive All-Ireland title – the only time before or since that this feat has been achieved.

1954: Players are forbidden from training full-time for matches.

1970: Matches are lengthened from 60 to 80 minutes for senior championship matches, but five years later are reduced to 70.

1971: The GAA abolish Rule 27 ('The Ban'), allowing its members to play or watch sports such as soccer and rugby.

1997: The championship is restructured so that the runners-up in the Munster and Leinster finals can still compete in the All-Ireland series.

2000: The number of substitutes is increased from three to five. Substitutes are now allowed for blood injuries.

All-Ireland Action

The first All-Ireland final was in 1887, when Galway and Tipperary togged out in a nearby inn and then played in front of just 5,000 fans. More than a century later the number of spectators might have increased but one thing has stayed the same – the passion of the occasion! Here are ten of the top finals ever played.

1900 Tipperary 2–5 London 0–6, Jones's Road (8,000)

The 1900 game was the first time a side from outside Ireland had competed in the final. It was a fast and furious game! London were trailing 0–5 to 0–3 at half-time but edged in front with less than five minutes remaining. But Mike Maher of Tubberdora inspired a late fightback and two frees took Tipp to glory.

1907 Kilkenny 3–12 Cork 4–8, Dungarvan (15,000)

Poet-priest J B Dollard threw in the sliotar and described what followed as 'a tremendous struggle'. Kilkenny trailed Cork by two goals at half-time but fought back with all their goals coming from Jim Kelly. In the closing minutes of the game Jack Anthony scored the point that clinched the title for the Marble County.

1922 Kilkenny 4–2 Tipperary 2–6, Croke Park (26,119)

One journalist who saw the final called it 'the best played in the hurling code in modern times'. With a three point lead and three minutes left on the clock, Tipperary seemed to be cruising to victory. However, Kilkenny refused to surrender and scored goals through Paddy Donoghue and Dick Tobin. Tipp nearly snatched a goal at the death but the sliotar went over the bar and Kilkenny were victorious.

1947 Kilkenny 0–14 Cork 2–7, Croke Park (61,510)

Rated by many as the greatest ever final, there was little to separate the sides at half-time although it was Kilkenny who held a narrow 0–7 to 0–5 advantage. Cork netted twice in the second period but Kilkenny's Terry Leahy kept his team in touch with three points. In the last minute Leahy sent over the winning point from 60m.

1956 Wexford 2–14 Cork 2–8, Croke Park (83,096)

With Cork's legendary Christy Ring going for a record ninth All-Ireland title, this was always going to be an unforgettable occasion and more than 80,000 fans were there to witness it. Nicky Rackard was in great form for Wexford, restoring their lead when Cork surged back in the second half. Ring nearly scored late on but the Model County's goalkeeper produced a sensational save.

The winners of the All-Ireland receive the Liam McCarthy Cup, named after a member of the GAA Congress, and first presented to Limerick when they beat Dublin in the 1921 final.

1968 Wexford 5–8 Tipperary 3–12, Croke Park (63,461)

One of the great comebacks in All-Ireland history! The final seemed to be Tipperary's when they went into the break up 1–11 to 1–3 thanks to Jimmy Doyle's goal. But Wexford came back in the second half and it was Tony Doran who inspired them with two goals. Tipp refused to die but a series of superb saves from 'keeper Pat Nolan ensured the cup went to Wexford.

1972 Kilkenny 3–24 Cork 5–11, Croke Park (66,137)

This final belonged to Eddie Keher who scored 2–9 and was responsible for a hair-raising comeback by Kilkenny. Eight points up with just twenty minutes to go, Cork believed they had the Liam McCarthy Cup in their grasp but Keher netted from 20 yards and then added another point. More points followed until Frank Cummins scored the clinching goal that broke the Rebels' hearts.

1990 Cork 5–15 Galway 2–21, Croke Park (63,954)

Galway found themselves a goal down in the first minute of the final but Cork fans soon realised the Tribesmen were fiercer than they looked. None more so than centre-forward Joe Cooney – he scored an amazing 1–6 to give Galway the lead at the interval, but Cork came back when John Fitzgibbon grabbed two late goals, finishing the match and leaving the fans breathless.

1994 Offaly 3–16 Limerick 2–13, Croke Park (54,458)

Limerick led by five points as the final whistle approached, prompting Offaly's Johnny Dooley to take a risk as he stood over a free. With his bench shouting at him to go for the point, Dooley ignored them and scored a stunning goal. Heartened by their team-mate's boldness, Offaly went on to score eight more points in an incredible five minutes to seize victory.

1997 Clare 0–20 Tipperary 2–13, Croke Park (65,575)

The first final between two teams from the same province (Munster) proved to be a classic that could have gone either way. Tipperary fought back in the second half with goals from Liam Cahill and Eugene O'Neill, but then Clare's Jamesie O'Connor came up with a crucial late point to send the Banner County wild.

John Fitzgibbon was the Cork hero in 1990

29

Midfield Maestros

They're the amazing all-rounders – the players who defend one minute and attack the next.

Tipp's Tommy Dunne leaves Kilkenny on the carpet

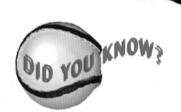

The legendary Nicky Rackard found fame as a full-forward with Wexford but he actually started out as a midfielder.

What have all midfielders got in common? Stamina; a big engine that allows them to keep running from the first minute to the last. Look at hurling's midfield maestros down the years, from the Cats' Frank Cummins to Tipp's Tommy Dunne, to James Fitzpatrick and Richie Murray – these lads weren't short of stamina!

Of course, there's more to being a masterly midfielder than just stamina. You need to have the tackling skills of a defender and a forward's eye for goal. A midfielder who can pick up points for his side is priceless.

The battleground for midfielders is the area around centre field. This is where games are often won and lost, because if one set of midfielders has control of the centre field they can act as the link between their defenders and attackers. At the same time, they can disrupt the opposition's supply of the sliotar.

Take Cork's back-to-back triumphs in the All-Ireland Championship in 2004 and 2005. On both occasions the Rebels' midfield duo of Jerry O'Connor and Tom Kenny won the midfield battle, and their side won the match.

The Dream Team

NO. 8

James 'Cha' Fitzpatrick
Midfield
KILKENNY

Born in Ballyhale, Fitzpatrick went to St Kieran's College and captained the side to the All-Ireland College title in 2003.

Fitzpatrick lined out for the Kilkenny senior side just one year later, and was in the Cats side which lost to Cork in the All-Ireland final. However, in 2006 the midfield marvel was a winner, taking titles in the National Hurling League, the Leinster Cup and the All-Ireland Senior Championship.

That same season he won his first All-Star award, and a second followed in 2007. In 2008 Fitzpatrick skippered the Cats to glory in the All-Ireland final against Waterford, scoring two points in the process on an unforgettable day.

 HAVE A HIT!

True or False?
Fitzpatrick was named Young Hurler of the Year in 2006.

NO. 9

Richie Murray
Midfield
GALWAY

The skilful 6ft Murray came of age during Galway's march to the 2005 All-Ireland final. He scored three points in the quarter-final upset over Tipperary. He was again on top form when the Tribesmen won a famous victory against Kilkenny in a memorable semi-final, and he was just 22 at the time!

Although Cork edged out Galway in the 2005 final it was clear that Murray had a bright future. A product of the St Thomas club, he has developed into one of the most effective midfielders in the game.

Richie Murray is a Galway Great

[True]

31

Catches Win Matches

It's true, catches really do win matches. One of the greatest hurling matches of recent years was Waterford's defeat of Cork in the 2004 Munster final.
In the final minute it seemed Cork were about to steal a last-gasp win but Waterford centre half-back Ken McGrath pulled off a sensational catch to save the Deise. Here's how to catch like Ken!

Chest catch

As the sliotar approaches, take your stronger hand off the hurley and hold it at chest height with your fingers cupped. Catch the sliotar in your cupped hand and then bring it into your chest for protection. Your hurley should not obstruct your catching hand but once you've caught the sliotar bring it across your body to shield the sliotar.

High catch

Take your stronger hand off the hurley as the sliotar approaches, but this time raise your cupped hand in the air with the palm facing out. Move towards the sliotar and when you are sure of its flight, jump up and catch the sliotar in your outstretched hand. If an opponent is jumping behind you, hold the hurley up and

James Walsh of Laois prepares to take the catch

behind you for protection, but if the opponent is in front of you, hold the hurley in front of the catching hand.

Training tips

Catching practice is fun and easy – and it doesn't matter if your friends aren't around. Stand a few metres in front of a wall (making sure there are no windows nearby!) with your hurley in one hand and the sliotar in the other. Throw the sliotar against the wall and catch the rebound. Change the height at which you throw the sliotar so that you practise low catches, chest catches and high catches.

Top Tipp

Winners of the very first All-Ireland title, the Premier County are still going strong over a century later!

Tipperary were the top dogs in hurling at the end of the 19th century. They managed to win five All-Ireland Championships in six years between 1895 and 1900.

Half a century later they ruled the sport once again as they claimed three-in-a-row starting with a hammering of Laois in the 1949 All-Ireland final. With a team that included the sensational Tony Reddan in goal and the hard-as-nails John Doyle in defence, few teams scored points against Tipp. They also had gifted Mick Ryan in attack.

Tipperary saw off Kilkenny in 1950, and a year later, topped Wexford in a thrilling final to claim a hat-trick of All-Ireland wins.

The next great Tipp team was the one which scooped four of the five All-Ireland Championships between 1961 and 1965. Jimmy Doyle and Babs Keating were lethal wingers in that side, while John Doyle was still as rock solid as ever at the back. Perhaps the most memorable of their four wins was the defeat of favourites Kilkenny in 1964 when Donie Nealon netted a hat-trick.

Although Tipperary haven't enjoyed the success of Cork or Kilkenny in recent seasons, they beat Galway to win a thrilling All-Ireland final in 2001 and still produce outstanding players such as Eoin Kelly, Brendan Cummins and Thomas Dunne.

DID YOU KNOW?

Tipperary won the first ever All-Ireland title in 1887 despite missing seven of their regular players because of a dispute over travelling costs.

Brendan Cummins is a top Tipp player

33

Best of the Rest

Cork, Tipp and Kilkenny may be hurling's 'Goliaths', but they've had their fair share of defeats over the years.

Clare beat Tipperary to win the 1997 All-Ireland title

Waterford and Kilkenny have met four times in the All-Ireland final, with the Deise losing three times, only triumphing in the 1959 replay.

Before the 1990s, Clare had only won the All-Ireland title once, in 1914. After a long wait, they scooped two wins in quick succession, first in 1995, and then two years later in a nail-biting encounter against Tipperary.

Like Clare, Offaly have only emerged as a powerful side in recent years. Their first All-Ireland medal was in 1981, and they've since won three more titles – 1985, 1994 and 1998. The 1998 victory was the most magical, with goals from Joe Errity and Brian Whelehan sending the Kilkenny Cats home to lick their wounds!

The 1980s was the decade when Galway stood up to hurling's Goliaths! Having previously won only one All-Ireland medal (1923), the Tribesmen lifted the Liam McCarthy Cup three times – in 1980, 1987 and 1988. Noel Lane was Galway's hero in the back-to-back wins, scoring goals that defeated both Kilkenny and Tipperary.

Limerick have won seven All-Ireland titles since their first victory in 1897. They reached the 2007 final but couldn't prevent Kilkenny getting their hands on the cup. Wexford have six medals to their name, including two on the trot in 1955 and 1956 when Nicky Rackard inspired them to glory against Galway and Cork.

The last time Dublin were All-Ireland champs was 1938, but between 1917 and 1927 they won the title four times, including victories over Cork in 1920 and 1927.

The Dream Team

HAVE A HIT!

True or False?
Shefflin scored eight points for the Cats in their thrashing of Waterford in the 2008 All-Ireland final.

NO. 11

Henry Shefflin

Centre half-forward

KILKENNY

One of the greats of the modern game, Shefflin has scored more championship points than anyone else in the game's history, except the incredible Eddie Keher.

He is the first player ever to win six consecutive All-Star awards (2002 to 2007) and the sharpshooter has also won the Hurler of the Year award twice.

Shefflin has won five All-Ireland medals and has a habit of rising to the big occasion. In the 2000 final he scored two goals, a feat he repeated in the 2002 defeat of Clare. He captained the Cats to victory in the 2007 final, scoring a first-half goal before departing at half-time with an injury.

'King' Henry Shefflin – one cool cat!

[True]

35

How to Speak Hurling

From puck-outs to pulls, all of hurling's funny phrases explained:

Free puck: Awarded when a defending player commits a foul inside his own 20m line but outside the large rectangle. It is taken from the 20m line opposite where the foul took place.

Penalty puck: Awarded to the attacking side for an aggressive foul within the large rectangle. Penalty pucks are taken from the centre spot of the 20m line and no more than three defending players may stand on the goal line.

Hopping: Players are allowed to run with the sliotar balanced on the hurley or with it 'hopping' on the stick.

Throw-in: The method of restarting the game.

Overcarry: When a player takes more than the permitted four consecutive steps while holding the sliotar in his hands.

Pucked: Another word for the throw-in, the method of starting or restarting the game.

Puck-out: When the attacking team scores or plays the sliotar over the end-line, play is restarted by a puck-out from the edge of the small rectangle.

65: When a defender sends the sliotar over his end-line the attacking side take a shot from the 65m line level where the sliotar went out of play.

Pull: To use the hurley to 'pull' an opponent while not making any attempt to play the sliotar. This penalty offence is punishable by a free puck.

Tackle: A player is allowed to make a side-to-side tackle for the sliotar provided at least one foot remains in contact with the ground and the opponent is in possession of the sliotar, playing it or moving towards it.

Toss: To 'toss' up the sliotar from the hand and hit it with the hurley, foot or hand.

The Dream Team

NO. 10

Eoin Kelly
Right half-forward
TIPPERARY

Tipperary's Eoin Kelly is every defender's nightmare with a killer instinct in front of goal. He made his Senior Championship debut in 2000 when he was only 18, and ever since Kelly has been one of hurling's hottest properties.

In 2001 he was part of the Tipp treble-winning side which scooped the National Hurling League title, the Munster Senior Hurling crown and the Liam McCarthy Cup. As if that wasn't enough, Kelly also collected his first All-Star award that year and won the Young Hurler of the Year!

More All-Star awards followed in 2002, 2004, 2005 and 2006, making Kelly only the second player in hurling history to have won five All-Stars at the tender age of 24.

[True]

True or False?
In his youth Eoin Kelly preferred to play in goal.

NO. 12

Dan Shanahan
Left half-forward
WATERFORD

Dan 'the Man' Shanahan made his senior debut for Waterford in 1998, although for the first few years he struggled to hold down a regular place in the Deise's starting 15. His breakthrough season came in 2004 when he scored a hat-trick of goals against Clare on the way to the Munster final.

In the final itself Shanahan found the net again as Waterford defeated Cork, and at the end of the season he was awarded his first All-Star. A second followed in 2006 and in 2007 he was part of the Deise side that won the National Hurling League title for the first time since 1963.

He then scored 3–3 as Waterford won the Munster title and he was voted 2007 Hurler of the Year, as well as winning a third All-Star.

Camogie Queens

Gaelic girls have been hurling for over 100 years. There are now more than 500 clubs with nearly 90,000 members, making camogie the queen of Irish sport!

The history of camogie (it gets its name from camóg, an alternative word for 'hurl') goes back to the start of the last century. The first ever game took place in 1904 at a Gaelic League Fair in Meath, and ever since there's been no stopping the rise of camogie.

Over the next twenty years more and more Gaelic girls took up the sport – with 32 counties starting clubs – but it wasn't until 1932 that the All-Ireland Senior Championship began. Dublin triumphed that year but it was Cork who won the first ever final played at Croke Park, when they beat Louth 4–3 to 1–4 in 1934.

Dubin were the dominant side for much of the 20th century, winning the All-Ireland title every year between 1949 and 1966, except in 1956! In recent years Cork and Tipperary have

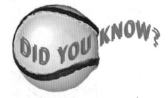

The winners of the Camogie All-Ireland Championship play for the O'Duffy Cup, named after Sean O'Duffy who helped establish the sport in the GAA.

ruled the roost until 2007, when the women of Wexford were crowned camogie queens. They beat Cork in the All-Ireland final thanks to two goals from Una Leacy.

Nearly 20,000 people saw Cork beat Galway in the 2008 Senior Camogie final – proof that camogie is more popular than ever! There are now over 500 clubs playing, with thousands of women hoping to one day become a star like Niamh Mulcahy of Limerick or Wexford's Kate Kelly.

Although camogie is very similar to hurling, there are some differences. In camogie the women play in skirts rather than in shorts, and the 'keeper wears the same coloured jersey as her team-mates.

Also, the sliotar in hurling is slightly bigger and heavier than its camogie cousin – but not by much!

Perhaps the biggest difference between the two sports is that in camogie players are allowed to hand-pass a goal, something which is forbidden in hurling. Conversely, the side-to-side charge (shouldering) is a foul in camogie and will earn you a ticking off from the referee!

Mary Leacy holds the O'Duffy Cup at the launch of the 2008 championship

Simply the Best

Brian Corcoran was the first player to win the Hurler of the Year award twice

Presented annually since 1958, the Hurler of the Year award honours the player considered to have been the star of that season's championship.

Brian Corcoran
Cork

The Rebel corner-back was named Hurler of the Year in 1992 aged only 18. Seven years later he made history by becoming the first player to win the award twice.

Henry Shefflin
Kilkenny

Named Hurler of the Year in 2002 and 2006, 'King Henry' was honoured for his inspirational displays for Kilkenny in winning the All-Ireland titles.

Seanie McMahon
Clare

One of the bravest centre-backs in the business, super Seanie was named Hurler of the Year in 1995 for helping the Banner County to their first All-Ireland title since 1914.

DJ Carey
Kilkenny

One of only three players to have won the Hurler of the Year award on two occasions, the Kilkenny star collected his first title in 1993 and added a second in 2000.

Dan Quigley
Wexford

A rock-hard defender, Dan won his award in 1968 having skippered the Model County to All-Ireland glory in an incredible comeback against Tipperary.

Joe Connolly
Galway

Joe was named Hurler of the Year in 1980 after he led the Tribesmen to their first All-Ireland title since 1923, a victory in which two of his brothers also shared.

Tommy Dunne
Tipperary

The Hurler of the Year in 2001, Tipp's Tommy Dunne not only led his side to All-Ireland victory but he also scored five points in the victory over Galway.

Ger Cunningham
Cork

Cork's goalkeeping great won three All-Ireland medals during his twenty-year career, including in 1986, the same season he was named Hurler of the Year.

Tony Wall
Tipperary

The Premier County legend won the first ever Hurler of the Year award in 1958 after he had captained his side to victory in that season's All-Ireland final.

Pat Delaney
Offaly

The big centre half-back was named Hurler of the Year in 1981 when Offaly came from behind to defeat Galway and claim their first All-Ireland title.

The Dream Team

NO.  13

Andrew O'Shaughnessy
Right corner-forward
LIMERICK

O'Shaughnessy showed his passion for points at an early age when he scored 2–8 (out of 2–10) for St Colman's College in the 2001 Colleges Cup final.

Ever since making his senior debut for Limerick in the 2003 Munster semi-final, 'Shocks' O'Shaughnessy has upped his image as a deadly finisher even if the Shannonsiders haven't always enjoyed national success.

That changed in 2007 when Limerick were runners-up in the Munster final and reached the All-Ireland final for the first time in eleven years. Though they lost to Kilkenny, O'Shaughnessy finished the season as the championship's top scorer and was rewarded with his first All-Star.

NO. 15

Joe Deane
Left corner-forward
CORK

Having won hurling titles at both school and university level, Deane was soon starring for the Cork U21 side, winning All-Ireland medals in 1997 and 1998.

In 1999 Deane was in sparkling form with the senior side as Cork won their first All-Ireland title in nine years. A great season was capped when Deane collected his first All-Star award.

Deane enjoyed more All-Ireland success with the Rebel County in 2004 and 2005 but a narrow defeat to Kilkenny in 2006 prevented a three-in-a-row triumph.

He fought back from illness in the winter of 2006 to captain Cork for the first time in 2007 and further success will surely come 'Deano's' way soon.

[True]

HAVE A HIT!

True or False? O'Shaughnessy is a soldier.

Hurling's Heroes

It's every fan's favourite pastime – coming up with the greatest team in history. We've thought of our fabulous fifteen, each one a hurling hero, but would they make it into your top team of all time?

1 Tony Reddan
goalkeeper
Tipperary

Named goalkeeper in the Team of the Millennium, Reddan won three consecutive All-Ireland medals with Tipperary (1949–52) and six National League titles.

2 John Doyle
right full-back
Tipperary

A hard man who played every championship match for Tipp during his nineteen-season career, Doyle won a record-equalling eight All-Ireland titles between 1949 and 1965.

3 Nick O'Donnell
full-back
Wexford

Born in Kilkenny but a Wexford legend, O'Donnell won three All-Ireland titles with the Model County in 1955, 1956 and 1960. He was also named Hurler of the Year in 1960.

4 Bobby Rackard
left full-back
Wexford

One of five brothers – another of whom was Nicky – Bobby was a brilliant defender who made his senior debut at 19 and won All-Ireland titles in 1955 and 1956 with Wexford.

5 Paddy Phelan
right half-back
Kilkenny

The grand-uncle of DJ Carey, Phelan played in seven All-Ireland finals and tasted success in four of them during the 1930s. He was also selected for the Team of the Millennium.

6 John Keane
centre-back
Waterford

Although he was named centre-back in the Team of the Millennium, Keane won his one and only All-Ireland title playing centre-forward with Waterford in 1948.

7 Brian Whelehan
left half-back
Offaly

One of hurling's coolest customers, Whelehan was a defender who could also play up front, as he showed in 1998 when he scored 1–6 as a full-forward in Offaly's All-Ireland triumph.

8 Jack Lynch
midfield
Cork

Famous as a hurler, footballer and politician, Jack was a stylish midfielder who played in all Cork's famous four-in-a-row All-Ireland victories from 1941 to 1945.

9 Lory Meagher
midfield
Kilkenny

Described as a 'magician' with a hurley, the legendary Lory won three All-Ireland titles with Kilkenny in the 1930s and proved himself a midfielder with pace and vision.

10 Christy Ring
right half-forward
Cork

Known as the greatest hurler of all time, Christy won a record eight All-Ireland titles in the 1940s and 1950s thanks to his combination of skill, strength and speed.

11 Mick Mackey
centre-forward
Limerick

Big and strong, Mick dominated Limerick hurling for nearly twenty years. He won his first All-Ireland medal in 1934 and led the Treaty County to two more victories in 1936 and 1940.

12 Nicky Rackard
left half-forward
Wexford

Though he won only two All-Ireland titles with the Model County (1955 and 1956), Nicky was a deadly finisher in front of goal and one of the stars of his generation.

13 Eddie Keher
left corner-forward
Kilkenny

Known for his fantastic free-taking, Keher won six All-Ireland titles between 1963 and 1975, and also scored an awesome 2–11 when Kilkenny lost to Tipp in the 1971 final.

14 DJ Carey
full-forward
Kilkenny

A goal-scoring sensation, Carey scored in three of his five triumphant All-Ireland final appearances and also collected nine All-Star awards between 1991 and 2002.

15 Jimmy Doyle
right corner-forward
Tipperary

Only 18 when he won his first All-Ireland title in 1958, Doyle skippered Tipp to more success in 1962 and 1965. He finished with six All-Ireland medals and six National League titles.

DJ Carey, the most recent player to make it into our team of legends

The Great Stadiums

The 'Croker' has witnessed some of hurling's grandest days

Hurling is home to some of Europe's finest stadiums: venues where the combination of atmosphere, colour and passion produces an unforgettable experience for both players and fans.

Croke Park, or the 'Croker' as it's known, was originally called 'Jones's Road'. In 1895 it hosted the first All-Ireland hurling final, in which Tipperary beat Kilkenny.

In 1913 the GAA bought the 14 acres of Jones's Road for £3,645 (about €340,000 today) and renamed it Croke Park in tribute to Archbishop Thomas Croke – an important personality in the early days of the GAA.

There wasn't much to the 'Croker' 100 years ago, just two small stands and some grassy banks, but over the years the GAA have transformed it into a breathtaking temple. The Hogan Stand was opened in 1924, the Cusack Stand in 1938 and the Nally Stand was built in 1952.

The GAA decided in the 1980s that the time had come to give Croke Park a complete overhaul and work began on modernising the stadium. It cost a whopping €265 million but the new-look

The first ever floodlit GAA match at Croke Park was in February 2007 when Dublin played Tyrone in the National Football League.

stadium – the fourth biggest in Europe – is one of the most magnificent arenas in the world. With a capacity of 82,500, Croke Park is a fitting venue for the action of All-Ireland day.

The other great hurling venue is **Semple Stadium** in Thurles, where the Munster final is held each season. The ground hosted its first such final in 1914 but it wasn't until 1968 that it was refurbished and renamed in honour of Tom Semple. He was a legendary Tipperary player, who led the Blues to All-Ireland glory in 1906 and 1908.

Galway's Pearse Stadium was given a makeover a few years ago and is now a handsome ground with a capacity of 34,000 and an all-weather playing surface.

The Gaelic Grounds in Limerick City was also updated recently to the tune of several million euro. With a 50,000 capacity it was money well spent, and the new-look stadium has clearly inspired the Shannonsiders because they reached the All-Ireland final in 2007 for the first time in eleven years.

Páirc Uí Chaoimh Stadium in Cork (named after a former secretary of the GAA) is another ground rich in history and it has been staging matches for over 100 years.

When Croke Park was modernised in the 1950s, its Hogan Stand was moved to the Gaelic Grounds where it stood until pulled down in the 1990s.

Semple Stadium has hosted many great matches

Fantastic Forwards

Forwards need to be fast – quick feet, quick hands and quick thinkers!

If opposition defenders are doing their job there won't be many clear-cut chances to score a goal during a match. So it's up to the forwards to take every chance that comes their way – even a half-chance.

One of the great strengths of the Cats' legend DJ Carey was his speed over the first 10m or so; he was so quick off the mark he usually left his defender for dead and then, smash! The sliotar was in the back of the net.

Eoin Kelly has wonderful vision and scores many of his goals by out-thinking defenders and anticipating a pass from a team-mate. By the time Kelly's marker has seen the danger, he's banged in three more points for Tipperary.

Every forward also needs to be able to strike the sliotar under pressure because often you get a clean sight of goal for just a second. Hesitate and you'll be blocked down. Work on your strikes at goal during training, concentrating on speed and accuracy, and don't forget to work on your weaker side as well as your stronger, dominant side.

If you can strike for goal from both the left and the right, it will cause all sorts of problems for the defence.

And remember, all the great forwards in hurling history, from Christy Ring to Nicky English to Henry Shefflin, have worked as part of a forward line. They weren't greedy or selfish, but they always looked to pass the sliotar to a team-mate if they thought he was in a better position to score.

Forwards today are not allowed to deliberately tackle the goalkeeper in the small square, but in the old days it was allowed for them to bundle the 'keeper into the net!

Nicky English (right) was a fantastic forward

The Dream Team

NO.

Joe Canning

Full-forward

GALWAY

Canning was a teenage sensation in Galway, winning honours for club and college before graduating to the Tribesmen U21 side in 2006. He helped them thrash Dublin to win the 2007 All-Ireland U21 title and that same season he scored ten points for his club, Portumna, as they beat Birr to win the All-Ireland Club Championship.

Blessed with great skills, Canning is a dead-ball specialist who was invited to tog out for the senior Galway side in 2006, but he declined, explaining that he needed more experience in the minor team. Now he has that experience Canning is sure to be one of hurling's hotshots in future years.

[False: Portumna]

True or False?
Canning was born in Dublin.

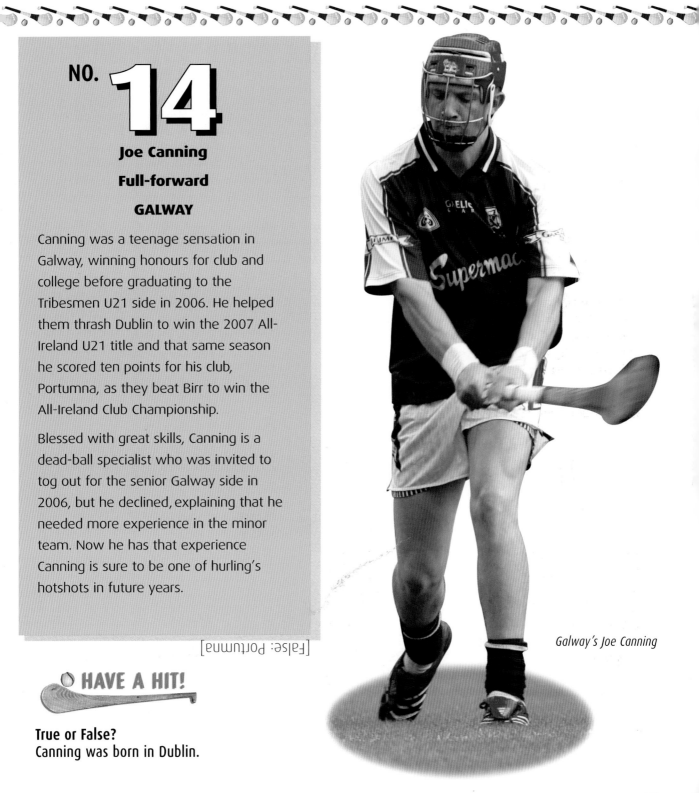

Galway's Joe Canning

The Record Breakers

In over a hundred years of hurling there have been some amazing records set by its stars. Some might be broken in years to come but others might remain forever – records that just can't be smashed!

The largest crowd at an All-Ireland final was the 84,856 spectators who crammed into Croke Park in 1956 to watch Wexford beat Cork.

Jack Lynch of Cork scooped six consecutive All-Ireland medals between 1941 and 1946. Incredibly, five were for hurling, but the sixth – in 1945 – was on the football field!

The first (and only) man to win All-Ireland medals for hurling and football in the same year was Cork's Teddy McCarthy, whose double delight came in 1990.

Cork and Kilkenny shared an unwanted record in 1999 when they took part in the first All-Ireland final to end without a goal being scored. Cork won 0–13 to 0–12, but it was a match most fans would prefer to forget.

Mick Gill won two All-Ireland winners' medals in 1924 – despite playing for different teams! How? He played for Galway in the 1923 season, but the final was postponed until early 1924. The following season he moved to Dublin and in December helped them win the title.

Kilkenny have appeared in the most All-Ireland finals (55), many of which they've won (31). Cork are next best, winning 30 of their 48 finals and Tipp have made it to Croke Park on 35 occasions.

Limerick won a record five consecutive National Hurling League titles between 1934 and 1938.

In 1989 Nicky English of Tipperary set a new scoring record in an All-Ireland final when he smashed a 2–12 in the 4–24 to 3–9 hammering of poor Antrim.

Nicky Rackard boasts the best points tally in a major championship match with an amazing 7–7 when Wexford whipped Antrim 12–17 to 2–3 in the 1954 All-Ireland semi.

Kilkenny's Noel Skehan is one of the best goalkeepers in hurling history and he's also the only man to have won nine All-Ireland medals. His first was in 1963, and his last came a staggering twenty years later!

1990 was a great year for Cork's Teddy McCarthy (left)